Maple Tree Press Inc.
51 Front Street East, Suite 200, Toronto, Ontario M5E 1B3
www.mapletreepress.com

Distributed in Canada by Raincoast Books
9050 Shaughnessy Street, Vancouver, British Columbia V6P 6E5

Distributed in the United States by Publishers Group West
1700 Fourth Street, Berkeley, California 94710

We acknowledge the financial support of the Canada Council for the Arts, the
Ontario Arts Council, the Government of Canada through the Book Publishing
Industry Development Program (BPIDP), and the Government of Ontario through the
Ontario Media Development Corporation's Book Initiative for our publishing activities.

ONTARIO ARTS COUNCIL
CONSEIL DES ARTS DE L'ONTARIO

Cataloguing in Publication Data
Lightfoot, Marge
        Cartooning for kids / written and illustrated by Marge Lightfoot.

ISBN 1-897066-38-4 (bound).   ISBN 1-897066-26-0 (pbk.)

    1. Cartooning—Technique—Juvenile literature. I. Title.

NC1320.L54 2005   j741.5   C2004-905352-3

Design & art direction: Word & Image Design Studio
Illustrations: Marge Lightfoot

Printed in China

F   G   H   I   J

Introduction

Want to share a funny story or a wacky idea? Pick up a pencil and draw a cartoon! It's a fun way to use your imagination.

Will your characters look real — or imaginary? Will your cartoon have words — or no words at all? Will it tell a joke in one frame, in a strip of frames — or will it go on for pages? It's all up to you. There are lots of different cartoon styles to choose from. Try out some of the cartoon styles in this book. Then pick the style you like best — or, better yet, create your own!

Not only will this book help you draw characters, it's also full of tips on how to create your own cartoons—from getting that great idea and putting it down on paper to coloring your cartoon and getting it ready to frame.

GETTING THE
Whole Picture

Let's take a quick look at the basic steps this cartoonist follows as he creates a cartoon.

1 First comes the idea.

2 The cartoonist picks up his pencil and sketches some sample characters.

3 Now he decides if he wants to tell his joke in one frame or in several frames.

Now that you have a general idea of what's ahead, let's look at each of these steps in more detail.

GETTING
Started

Ready to start cartooning? Don't worry—you don't even need a pencil and paper. Many great cartoonists begin a cartoon by doing a little creative daydreaming. You may find that's where some of your best ideas come from.

Try getting ideas by reading books, magazines, newspapers, and comic books. Heard any silly or unusual stories lately? Maybe you can turn one of them into a cartoon. Become a people-watcher or think about your own real-life experiences. Is there a cartoon you'd like to draw about a funny thing that happened to your family?

Always jot down your ideas when you think of them, so you don't let any good ones get away.

▲ Save all your cartoon ideas in a little pocket-sized notebook.

① HEY! WHO TOOK MY FOOD!
② NO! THIS IS NOT A BIRD BATH!
③ AREN'T YOU SUPPOSED TO BE MIGRATING?
④ I DON'T CARE IF YOU ARE A CAT BIRD!
THIS IS MY DINNER!

Thought of some great captions for a cartoon? Keep some recipe cards handy for jotting them down. Use the blank side of the card for sketching illustration ideas. Keep all your cards together in a recipe box.

TRANSPORTATION
PEOPLE SPORTS
HOLIDAYS LANDSCAPES
ANIMALS COSTUMES
PICTURE FILE

Clipping and filing pictures from old newspapers, magazines and catalogs can give you cartoon ideas—and you can use them for help in drawing people, tigers, sailboats, evergreen trees and other parts of your cartoons.

Having trouble coming up with a good idea? Some cartoonists find it helps to just plunge right in and start doodling whatever pops into their heads— a setting, some stick characters, a funny-looking object and so on.

Sometimes, seeing the doodles on a page helps *the* cartoonist come up with a great joke or a funny situation.

TIP!

Try placing a thin book or a piece of plywood on your lap and leaning it against your desk or table to create a more comfortable, angled drawing surface.

Give doodling a try and see if it works for you.

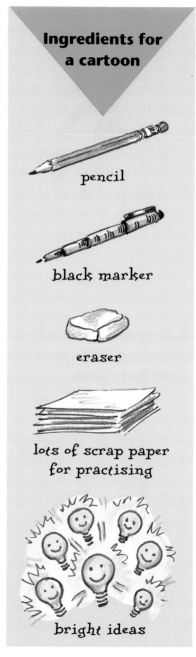

Ingredients for a cartoon

pencil

black marker

eraser

lots of scrap paper for practising

bright ideas

Many cartoonists like to let their ideas sit for a while. Wait for a few days after you've written down your ideas and then take a look at them again. Is there one you like best? Maybe it's time to try it out. Draw a few rough sketches of your cartoon idea. Stick figures are okay at this stage.

Don't get stuck on one way of illustrating your idea. Make a lot of rough, quick drawings, then choose the sketches you like best.

Plan your cartoon in pencil. Then trace the pencil lines with ink or black marker. When the ink or marker is completely dry, erase the pencil.

You can draw any type of characters in your cartoon: realistic-looking people or wacky ones, animals that live on Earth or ones from another planet, even objects that speak and move!

TIP!

Kneaded rubber erasers are the best kind to use. You can shape them, just like Plasticine, into thin points to erase tiny areas of your cartoon without erasing the parts you like. And they won't leave eraser crumbs on your paper.

DRAWING
People

circles

ovals

squares

HEADS AND FACES

Ready to draw some cartoon people? Let's start with their heads and faces. You can use the shape of a person's head to show something about personality, and the expression on a face to show what the person is feeling.

Cartoon people can have heads in almost any shape. Trace these simple shapes or draw your own. Take a look at all these different ways to draw eyes, noses, mouths, ears, eyebrows and hair. Trace these features, then experiment with creating new faces. What happens when you draw a face and then change the shape of the head? Try it!

pear shapes

rectangles

triangles

Be creative! Have some fun adding heads and faces to make fingerprint people.

TIP! **Eyebrows always add expression.**

For inspiration, go for a walk and take a good look at the variety of faces that you see around you. Look at people's eyes, noses, mouths and the shapes of their heads. Do a quick sketch of them in your notebook. Don't forget to draw their hair!

There are lots of different styles of cartoon characters. Try drawing both "cartoony" and more realistic characters.

Be a cosmetic surgeon! Tape tracing paper over a photo of a face from a magazine, a newspaper or your own photo collection and trace it. Then change the original by adding a big nose, beady eyes, bushy eyebrows or whatever you like.

11

Heads move and tilt in different ways. When you draw a head, think of it as a ball on an axis, like a globe of the world on a stand.

Tracing these heads will help you learn how to draw faces in all kinds of positions.

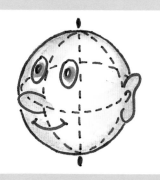

1 Divide the head with four lines that run from top to bottom and an equator that runs around it.

2 Draw the nose in the middle where the lines cross.

3 The ears go on the sides where the lines cross.

4 The eyes go above the nose. The mouth goes below the nose.

When your brothers and sisters are watching television, practise drawing their profiles. Is your mother looking down while she reads? Sketch the position of her head.

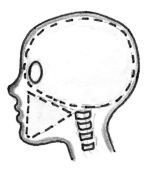

◄ **A human skull is made up of a triangle and an egg-shape that sticks out at the back.**

BODIES

A head starts from a simple shape. So does a body! With a pencil, draw the simple shape of a character. Then add shapes for the arms and legs. See how some of the shapes overlap here? This helps get everything in the right place. Now erase the lines you don't want.

Look at me! A cartoonist drew me by putting together simple shapes.

a circle for the head

a pear shape for the body

ovals for long, straight bones

triangles for the feet

Turn *the* golfer's pear-shape body upside-down to create a different kind of body for this weightlifter.

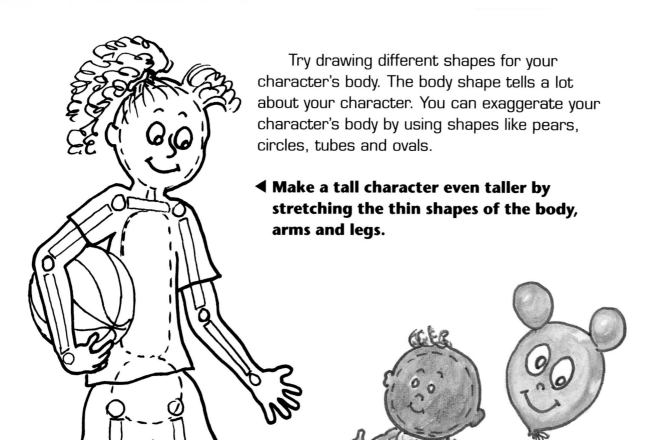

Try drawing different shapes for your character's body. The body shape tells a lot about your character. You can exaggerate your character's body by using shapes like pears, circles, tubes and ovals.

◄ **Make a tall character even taller by stretching the thin shapes of the body, arms and legs.**

▲ **Make a baby even cuddlier by drawing circle shapes for his body and head. Drawing the head quite large will also help your character look more babyish.**

Draw a person using:

1 pear shape

1 circle

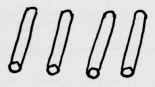

4 pipe shapes

2 triangles

Now add a face and hands!

MOVEMENT

Want your character to come alive? Then get your character moving with an action line! An action line is a single pencil line drawn down the middle of the cartoon character's body that shows the basic movement of the body. See how the action line shapes these characters as they leap, glide, stretch and tuck?

When you plan a character's pose, try lightly penciling in an action line. You can erase it after it helps you put a sense of movement into the character's pose.

Spines are flexible. They are part of the action line. See how the spines of these moving characters curve and bend?

Here's how you can add more detail to your moving character.

Use the "Pause" control on a video cassette recorder to freeze action so you can sketch it. Ask a friend to take turns "freezing" in an action pose so you can both practise drawing movement.

Bones meet at joints. The joints allow the many parts of our bodies to move in different directions. Check out the ways in which your joints move. It'll help you when you draw your cartoon characters in action.

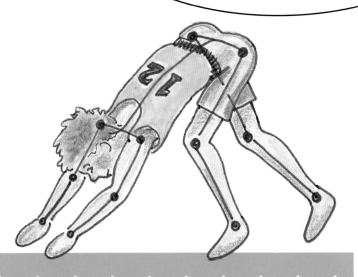

Plan your character's shape using dots for the joints and lines for the bones. Add ovals for the head, hands and feet. Then sketch in a rough outline for the body and add a face and hair.

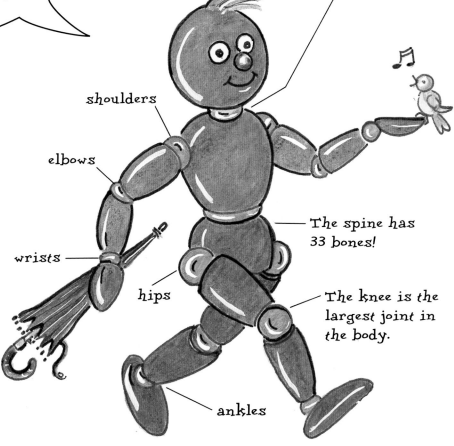

The neck is part of the flexible spine.

shoulders

elbows

wrists

hips

The spine has 33 bones!

The knee is the largest joint in the body.

ankles

16

See how the spine curves? The action line follows the direction of the dive—up, and then out and down.

Trace photos of people in action, and fill in lines and dots for bones and joints. Remember to draw the flexible spine. It is usually curved in the direction the person is moving. Extend it and it will turn into an action line.

Where will the action of your character take place? Is your character running on the grass? Springing from a diving board? Kicking a ball? Sketch the grass or diving board or ball before you draw your character; this helps you know just where to put your character in the scene and helps you draw the body pose just right.

•••• ARMS AND LEGS

You've practised drawing heads and faces, basic body shapes and bodies in motion. Now try sketching other parts of the body, such as arms and legs.

Here are some examples of realistic ones . . .

and some not so realistic ones!

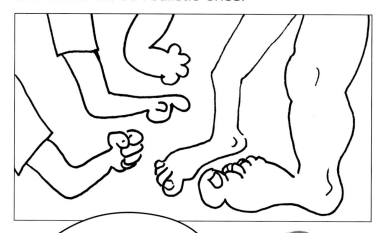

I'm a great model because you can arrange my body in many action poses. Look at how my arms and legs bend!

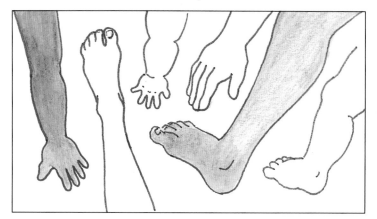

See how changing the action line and the position of a sad character's arms and legs turns her into a happy character?

You may want to buy a wooden mannequin at an art store.

HANDS AND FEET

Almost every cartoon character you'll draw—realistic or not—will have hands! Simple shapes work together to make hands.

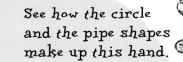

See how the circle and the pipe shapes make up this hand.

Draw the entire hand first, then add the object that the hand is holding. Erase the lines you don't need.

Use your hand as a model. ▶

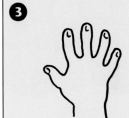

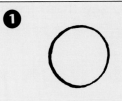

❶

Start with a circle -

❷

and add slim pipe shapes for fingers.

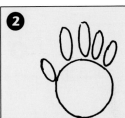

❸

Now flatten one side of the hand and use an eraser to turn the pipe shapes into fingers. Add finger nails if you want.

When you see them from the side, feet look like triangles with toes.

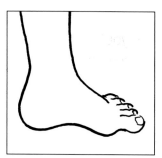

1 Start with a triangle. Round the sharp edges.

2 Toes are ovals all in a row—one big and four small.

3 Give the triangle some shape. Then erase the lines you don't need. Add toe nails if you want.

Imagine what the rest of this character might look like. Draw the character— from the feet up!

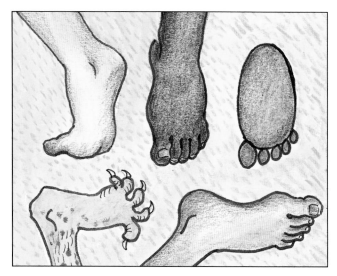

An oval foot and oval toes become a foot with an instep and an ankle.

You may want to draw a character's feet from other angles too, like these ones.

What you draw on your cartoon character's feet tells a lot about the character.

Be sure to save pictures of feet and footwear in your picture file.

A COMPLETE WARDROBE

What type of clothing would help the reader get to know your character?

Draw the rough outline of your character's body. If you want the clothes to look tight, draw them right over the body lines. If you want them to appear loose, use your outline of the character's body as a hanger to put the clothes on.

Characters' jewelry, tools, equipment, accessories and hairstyles also help to introduce the characters to the reader.

Photocopy your favorite photos of people. Cut out the faces and glue them to some drawing paper. Practise changing the personality, the age or the occupation of the person by drawing clothes of your choice.

See how the sleeves follow the top of the boy's arms, but sag underneath his arms?

TIP! **It's important to plan your cartoon character's wardrobe.**

Here are some cartoon characters with wardrobe tips for you.

My simple clothes are drawn with just a few strokes of the pencil! See how the wrinkles are added where the fabric folds?

I'm ready to leave the beach now. Please cover me with some tracing paper and draw some clothes for me to wear to the office.

How about giving me some more hair while you're at it?

Tra-la-la . . . Wavy lines make my gown look billowy.

My clothes are rugged for riding. Draw stitching along the seams to show that my pants are jeans.

STEP-BY-STEP REPLAY

You've come a long way—from drawing simple shapes to drawing cartoon characters! Here are some step-by-step guidelines to help you put together all that you've learned.

2

What do you want your character's action line to look like? Will your character be running? Jumping? Falling down?

3

1

Think about the character you want to draw. Then start by putting together some simple shapes.

What kind of face do you want your character to have? One of these?

Erase the lines you don't need and smooth out the basic shape a little.

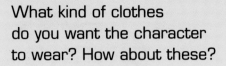

What kind of clothes do you want the character to wear? How about these?

5

Erase some more lines . . .

7

or these?

6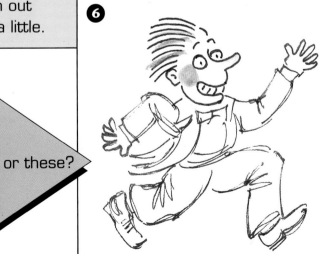

and add any final details. Now put down your pencil and take a look. Do you like the result?

8

DRAWING
Animals

pear shape

square

•••••• HEADS

A cartoon character doesn't have to be a person. Animals make great cartoon characters—and their faces can tell a reader a lot about their character too. Draw some simple shapes and turn them into cartoon animal heads. Use as many different shapes as you can.

triangle

Use the tips for drawing people's heads, faces and expressions when you're drawing animal characters too.

circle

A few extra lines and you can add whiskers, antennae, a mane or feathers.

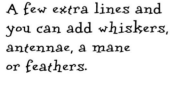

 TIP! Animals have hairstyles too! Place tracing paper over the heads you've drawn and turn a line into many short lines. It's a great way to create fur!

BODIES

Animals are many different shapes and sizes. Start with drawing the basic body shape. Add the head. What shape are the animal's legs? Add other simple shapes to complete your cartoon animal.

Overlap the basic shapes to draw the animal you want. Erase the lines you don't want. Smooth out the shapes.

Add a pattern to make a butterfly look real.

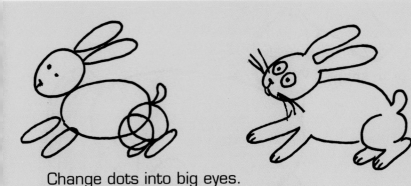

Change dots into big eyes.

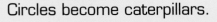 

Circles become caterpillars.

Lots of simple shapes add up to amazing cartoon animals!

oval

pear shape

See how the shapes can overlap?

half circles

rectangles

lines

pear shape

circle

oval

pipe shapes

circle

triangles

MOVEMENT

Animals move in different ways than people do. Can you spot their joints? That may help you draw them in action.

Look at the way this bird's wings lift.

Look how the action line springs up!

Eyes are big.

Bushy tail is up.

Some monkeys' tails are very flexible!

Hair is on end.

Mouth is open.

Claws are out and ready for action!

See how the giraffe's neck can bend?

29

Can you see how the elephant's trunk curls like a fire hose? Draw wrinkles where the skin bends.

Look at the way this dog's back bends as the dog runs.

Look closely at the way the camel's hind legs can bend. Do a few quick sketches of a horse's hind legs. You can start by tracing these legs.

30

SPECIAL TOUCHES

Think about the habits of the animal character you want to draw. Can this animal do something that no other animal can? Try highlighting some of its most outstanding features. Does the animal look funnier this way?

Armadillos roll up into a ball *to protect themselves.*

Kangaroos have pouches. What can you put in your cartoon kangaroo's pouch?

Dress up a cartoon animal.

Clothes help create a personality.

DOUGHNUTS TO GO

PLACE ORDER

Cartoon animals don't have to be real.

CARTOON CLUES

You can make your characters speak without words. Use symbols and body positions to give the reader clues about how your character feels.

Look at the body language of these people. They lean toward one another and smile sweetly. The cartoonist has added hearts to tells us they are in love.

See how this dog's tears are exaggerated to show how sad he is? He droops and his shoulders slump. The broken heart emphasizes just how sad he is!

Use your finger to trace an action line through the elephant.

How can you tell this person is afraid? Look at the exaggerated beads of sweat flying from him! See the speed streaks at his back and the dust puffs at his feet? Try using simple lines like these to help create the idea that your character is running quickly.

There's no doubt about it—this elephant is startled! Everything about this elephant is moving upward: its ears, legs, trunk and tail. Its whole body is in the air. See how the cartoonist has emphasized this by leaving a space between the character's feet and its shadow on the ground?

ADDING
Texture

Hey, these things really work!

• • • • • • LINES

Here are a few tips on using markers to give your cartoon characters some extra personality!

There are the kind of markers you use at school and there are fine-quality ones that you can buy at art stores. So that you can easily color in both small and large areas of your cartoon, markers have fine points, medium points and wide points.

A good marker to use for drawing cartoons is a waterproof all-purpose marker with a medium point. For thin strokes and details use fine-point markers. For wide strokes and strong-looking lines use markers with wider tips. But experiment with all types of markers until you find the ones you prefer.

For a more interesting cartoon, combine thick and thin lines using different-size markers.

 TIP! **Store your markers in a plastic bag and they won't dry out.**

PATTERNS

Experiment with ways to use your pencils, pens and markers to create different patterns. Use their tips and the sides of the tips. Make swirls, blots and curlicues. Draw lines close together or far apart, or cross them.

lines

spots

wood

broken hatching

cross-hatching

curls

solid black

tissue

See how shading makes the horse's left rear leg look farther away from you than its right rear one?

COLOR

Now that you've drawn characters in pencil and then in ink or marker, why not start to experiment with color? Try using colored pencils, colored markers and watercolors.

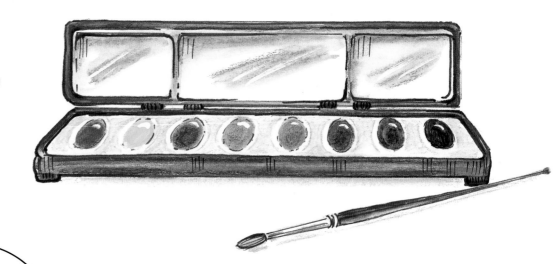

Store your dry brushes in an upright position to keep the bristles straight and smooth.

Watercolor paint will make regular marker run. If you want to color your cartoon with watercolor paints, draw it first with a waterproof black marker.

Watercolors can be blended to make different skin tones. So can colored pencils. Try covering one color with another and see what happens.

Always wash your brushes in water when you are finished painting with them. Lay your brushes flat to dry.

Typewriter-correcting fluid can't be colored over, but an artist's paint called graphic white can. Use it to make changes to your marker, ink and watercolor cartoons.

Here's how:

1 Squeeze a small amount of graphic white onto a dish.

2 Wet a small brush. Squeeze the water out of the bristles so they are damp, not dripping wet. Dip the brush in the graphic white and gently paint over the lines you want to erase.

3 Let it dry. Can you still see the lines you are trying to cover up? Add another coat and let it dry again. Several thin coats of white work better than a thick, blobby coat.

4 When the white is completely dry, draw over it with pencil, marker, ink or watercolor.

TIP! You can also cover marker mistakes with a little white tempera paint. Remember to keep the lid on tight or the paint will dry out quickly.

GUESS WHO!

SETTING THE
Scene

By now, you've thought of some characters and practised drawing them. Think for a moment about a joke or a story you want to tell. Do you want to add some detail to your cartoon to show the reader where it's taking place?

Maybe you'll get some ideas when you look at these simple, easy-to-recognize settings. Certain key objects in these settings help make each scene look familiar to the reader.

TIP!

❶ **When creating a scene, use a pencil or marker to draw the whole thing as best as you can.**

❷ **Want to make some changes? Place tracing paper over top and trace your favorite parts into a different place in the scene. Leave off the parts you don't like.**

Desert

Simple lines and dots create sand. Add a cactus or some tumbleweed. Doesn't a sun drawn like this look much hotter than a sun drawn with lines for rays?

Winter

Draw a snowman, snowflakes and some snow drifts. A few lines create a chilling wind.

Tropical Paradise

Draw a line shaped like a horse-shoe for a shoreline. Add a distant mountain ridge, a swaying palm tree, dots for sand, a bright sun and a cruising sailboat.

Doctor's Office

Check your photo file to help you draw in details such as a medical diploma, an examining table and other medical equipment.

Wilderness

Draw a series of jagged lines for mountains, then add snow-capped peaks, trees and birds. A few lines make the lake look calm.

Farm

Draw a meadow, farm animals and a barn. Add a tractor and perhaps a haystack. A fence is two long lines with short lines running through them.

To get ideas for background scenes, carry a sketchbook and draw what you see around you. Keep your pictures to use later.

Now, try creating some of those key objects that help the reader recognize a scene. Remember how you thought about shapes when you were drawing people and animals? Well, try the same thing for drawing objects!

Try looking at an object from a distance to draw its basic shape. Then take a closer look when you're ready to add details.

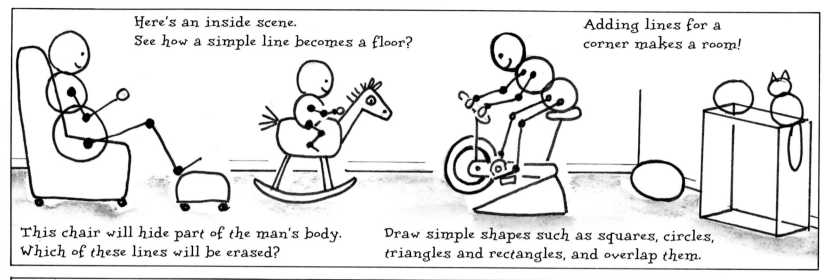

Here's an inside scene.
See how a simple line becomes a floor?

Adding lines for a corner makes a room!

This chair will hide part of the man's body. Which of these lines will be erased?

Draw simple shapes such as squares, circles, triangles and rectangles, and overlap them.

Adding a pattern and an arm to the armchair finishes it off!

Shadows anchor objects to the ground.

See how the rocking horse doesn't change much? It's just shapes joined together. A few lines give it movement.

Imagine that you want the action in your cartoon to take place outside on a city street corner. What details will help to show this setting?

TIP! Leave enough room for speech balloons if your characters need to speak in your joke (see page 43). Then add the details of the setting around them.

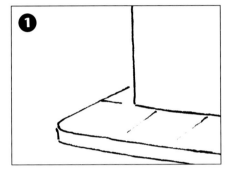

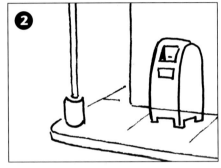

❶ Here's a building, a sidewalk and a street. With just these few lines, the reader can already see where the character might stand.

❷ Draw some common objects in the scene, like a pole and a mailbox.

❸ Place your character in the scene, then add details like a drain in the road and bricks on the wall.

❹ When the ink is dry, add color. Shadows are the final touch.

If the characters are more important to your cartoon than the setting, place them in the picture first.

Can you think of something funny that might happen in this scene? Draw another scene to show what could happen next.

Want to draw an unfamiliar scene? Search through your picture files for ideas.

TELLING
Your Joke

····· VISUAL GAGS

Okay, now you have your characters and your scene. How about putting them together to tell your joke? Don't worry if you don't get it right the first time. Do a few more rough sketches until your cartoon works.

In a visual gag cartoon, such as this one, the picture tells the whole story. It doesn't need any words. When you draw your cartoon, draw the most important character in heavy, bold lines so that the character will stand out. Draw the less important details in fine lines.

TIP! **Can't come up with a joke to tell? Look through the cards in your idea file.**

• • • CAPTIONS OR SPEECH BALLOONS

How can you tell whether or not your cartoon needs words? Try it with them and without them. Sometimes it can be hard for you to know which works best, since you created the cartoon. Ask a friend or two to read it both with and without the words; then ask which cartoon works best.

This cartoon is just as funny without any words.

TIP! Want to draw a box or frame for your cartoon? Place the cardboard mat from an old picture frame on your paper and trace around the inside edge.

If you decide your cartoon needs some words to be understood best, make room in your cartoon frame for a speech balloon or two.

But what if the frame is full of action and the words get in the way? No problem! Write the words spoken by your character underneath in a caption. Spoken words need quotation marks around them — and make sure the character speaking has his mouth open!

OSCAR NEVER SEEMED TO KNOW WHEN "HIDE AND SEEK" WAS OVER.

WHOOSH!

"QUIET! THIS IS A SCHOOL ZONE!"

A caption can also be a description or explanation of what is happening, like in this example.

Before you print your caption under your cartoon, practise writing it on another piece of paper. Read it over a few times. Can you make it any shorter? A short, snappy caption often works better than a long one. It fits better underneath your cartoon frame, too!

LETTERING

It's important that the reader be able to read the words in your cartoons! Try this method for printing neatly.

Start off by using a simple letter style, like this, for both captions and speech balloons:

Experiment with other styles, but test them by asking your friends or family members to read your lettering.

TIP!

ABCDEFGHIJKLMNOPQRSTUVWXYZ

Printing words inside speech balloons can be tricky. Sometimes, it takes careful planning for the words to fit. If you follow these tips, you'll be able to create speech balloons that fit perfectly in your cartoons.

❷ Place tracing paper over your cartoon and on it write your caption. Do you like the way it sounds? Is the message clear? Lightly draw a balloon around your words. Does the caption fit inside your cartoon?

❶ Draw a rough sketch of your cartoon. Think about what you want your characters to say.

3 Remove the tracing paper. Above the character's head, use a ruler to draw in one set of parallel lines for every line you want the character to say.

4 Lightly pencil in the words of the speech between the parallel lines.

5 When the words fit, trace over them with a fine-point or medium-point marker.

Don't forget to show who each speech balloon, belongs to!

After you have printed your caption, add the balloon around your words.

6 In pencil, draw the speech balloon around the words.

DON'T CROWD LETTERS INTO A TINY LITTLE BALLOON !!

ALWAYS GIVE YOUR LETTERS PLENTY OF AIR SPACE !!

7 Trace the speech balloon in marker. Wait at least 20 minutes for the marker to dry; then erase the pencil.

TIP! Leave plenty of space between the words and the speech balloon so they will be easy to read.

OTHER USES FOR BALLOONS

Balloons can contain other things besides your characters' words. Put symbols for sounds or feelings in balloons!

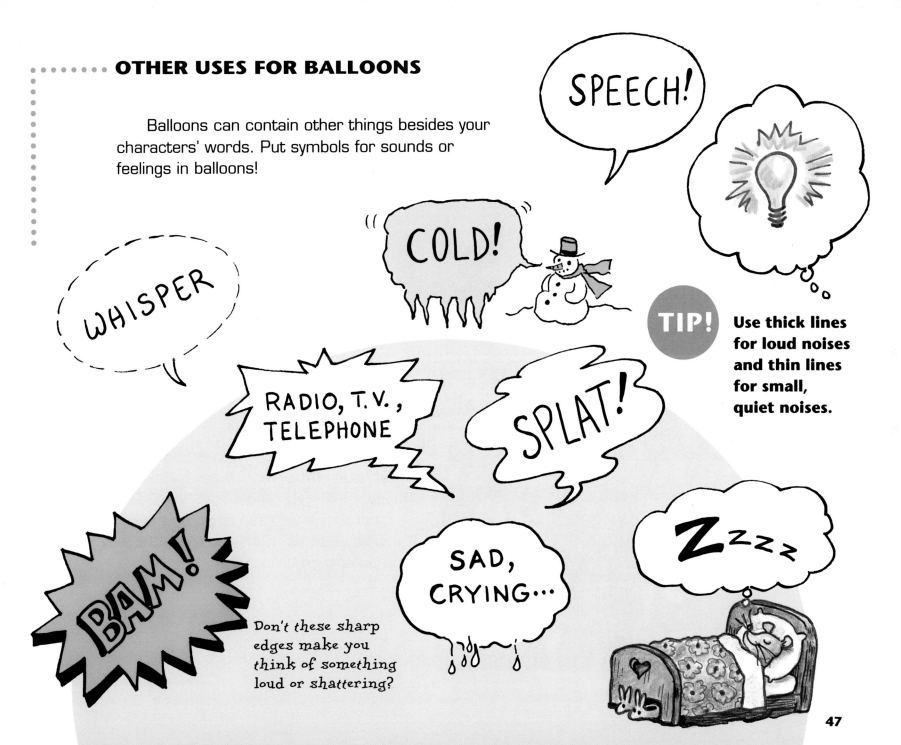

SPEECH!

COLD!

WHISPER

RADIO, T.V., TELEPHONE

SPLAT!

TIP! **Use thick lines for loud noises and thin lines for small, quiet noises.**

BAM!

Don't these sharp edges make you think of something loud or shattering?

SAD, CRYING…

Zzzz

ARRANGING BALLOONS

How do you know where to place the balloons in your cartoons? It can be tricky, but here are a few basic guidelines to follow so your cartoons will be easily understood.

When there's only one balloon, it's easy for the reader to know what to read first.

But what about when there are two balloons? Or three?

Do you like the way these cartoons are planned? Can you easily understand what was going on in the frames?

Probably not. The speech balloon on the left side of the frame wasn't spoken first, but you most likely read it first. Why? Because most things we read begin on the left and continue to the right—so that's the way we read speech balloons!

Is this one on the left any better? Probably, but look at the one below it. It's the easiest to read. See how the position of the characters has been switched so that the first speaker is on the left side of the frame now?

When you have three characters talking in the same frame, plan who speaks first, second and third, and arrange them in the frame in those positions. See how much better this reads now?

Speech balloons aren't always arranged from left to right. Sometimes they are arranged one above the other. Which would you read first? Probably the top one! So be sure to place the first speech balloon on top when you design your speech balloons this way.

BEYOND ONE FRAME

Some cartoon stories or jokes just can't be told in one frame. They need more frames to show action and change. Some need an entire strip of frames! Cartoon strips and cartoon books have one main thing in common: they both have a beginning, a middle and an end.

Let's create a cartoon strip step by step. Think of an idea for a cartoon story, and then try to write it in three parts: the beginning, the middle and the end.

Draw three boxes. Lightly sketch in the characters, speech balloons and scene details in pencil for each part of your cartoon.

The beginning frame sets the scene, introduces the cartoon characters and starts the action.

The middle frame continues the action and builds excitement for the reader.

The end frame delivers the joke or the conclusion to the story. For the reader, it's like the answer to a puzzle.

Sometimes a cartoon works best when the reader sees everything together in one frame. But some cartoons need more than one frame for all the action and suspense. The best way to figure out if your cartoon joke or story needs more than one frame is to draw your cartoon both ways. Sketch your cartoon in one frame and then spread it over two or three frames. Which works better?

Look at the single frame cartoon. Now look at how it has been expanded into two frames. Which do you like better? Why? Think about your answers to these questions when you plan your own cartoons.

To add interest to your cartoon strips, try combining frames with speech balloons and frames without speech balloons.

BEYOND THREE FRAMES

Maybe your cartoon is like one of the color comics that you can read in the weekend newspaper—it just won't fit in three frames! When your cartoon is long, there's more room to add detail; but remember that it still has to have a beginning, a middle and an end. A long cartoon is more challenging to create because each frame has to be interesting enough to keep the reader reading!

You can set up your long cartoon in frames like this or design your own format.

1 ▼ Most strips start with the title in the upper left-hand corner.

3 Now the real story starts ... ▶

5 adding excitement... ▶

2 This *throw-away section introduces the scene,*
▼ *but it isn't too important to the action of the
story. It's called the throw-away section because
if there isn't enough room for the whole cartoon
in a newspaper, this frame could be thrown away!*

Think of a comic book as a weekend funny that goes on and on and on! The characters in some comic books are so interesting, they star in comic book after comic book. Think about the characters when you're reading comic books, and try to figure out what makes you want to know more about them. How does the cartoonist keep you turning the pages to find out what happens next?

Interested in making your own comic book? First develop a cast of characters. Then in pencil draw their adventures on loose paper or in a school notebook. When you have the pages planned out and the action in place, transfer your sketches to comic book pages, and trace them in marker.

◀ **4** *and continues ...*

◀ **6** *and, finally, the joke
or conclusion,
in the last box.*

TIP!

Don't forget to add a title and a cover that makes everyone want to read your comic book!

CHANGING ANGLES

Here are some tips for making your cartoons the best that they can be! Before you draw the strip, stop and think carefully about each frame. It helps to pretend you're a film director. "Direct" each frame as if it's a scene you're shooting through a camera.

Each frame in this comic strip is drawn from the same angle. We see the characters in the same position in each frame, and the setting doesn't change either.

Just as a director shoots from different angles, you can draw your scenes as if you're looking at them from different angles. By changing the way the reader views a scene, you can make the scene more dramatic.

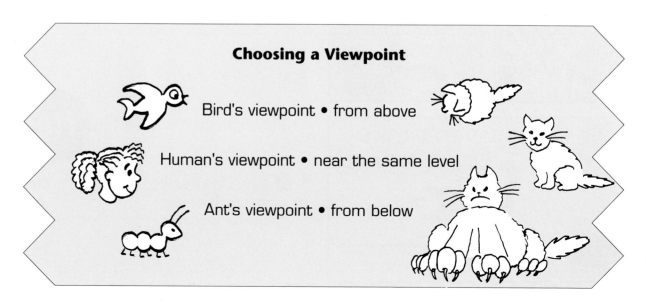

Choosing a Viewpoint

Bird's viewpoint • from above

Human's viewpoint • near the same level

Ant's viewpoint • from below

Think about the scene you want to draw. Would it look best from a straight-on view, as if the reader is looking directly at it—like this?

What if it were drawn as if the reader were looking at it from above—like this?

Or below—like this?

When you use these angling techniques you can make the reader feel either very tall or very small. Would this make your joke or story more effective? Think about trying out these techniques when you create your scenes.

TIP!

Practise drawing from a bird's view by drawing an object you see on the ground from the second floor of a building. Then, practise drawing from an ant's view by drawing objects on a shelf high above you.

A director's camera can back away for a long shot or zoom in for a close-up shot. A long shot can remind the reader of the setting. It can remind the reader that the characters are part of a larger scene. A close-up shot can zoom in on facial expressions and make an exciting scene even more exciting!

Explore new ways of looking at things. Do you think drawing this scene close-up and from this low angle makes the reader feel like part of the action?

Draw your characters in the distance to show the setting.

Silhouettes add variety and drama! See how a new setting is created?

This close-up lets us see the characters' expressions.

PHOTOCOPYING

How can you make your finished cartoon look polished? It's easy! Just like magic, a photocopier can reproduce your cartoon in seconds, giving you a clean, crisp copy. Just remember—before photocopying, carefully erase all the pencil smudges, and use graphic white or white tempera paint to cover up any lines you don't want to show.

Most photocopying is done in black-and-white, but for a little extra expense you can get your favorite color cartoons reproduced. Also, some photocopiers can reduce or enlarge the size of your cartoon.

Be sure to show your cartoons to people. Perhaps your school or club newsletter would like to publish some of your best ones. Frame a favorite cartoon for a special friend. A comic book with a friend as a main character makes a great birthday gift. The next section in this book will give you some more ideas for ways to share your cartoons!

▲ Tape

▲

I MADE IT ESPECIALLY FOR YOU!

THANKS... I LOVE IT!

Why not store some of your favorite cartoons in a large envelope or a homemade folder of poster paper or cardboard? As time goes by, you'll enjoy looking through your collection and seeing how your drawing style changes and develops. You'll also see how your sense of humor grows!

OTHER
Cartoon
Projects

•••••••• GREETING CARDS

Use your new talent for drawing cartoons to make your own greeting cards. Sending a card is a great way to help celebrate a birthday, special anniversary, a graduation or a holiday, or just to keep in touch with a friend.

Make cards out of heavy paper, such as sketchpad paper, construction paper, poster paper and cardboard, or brown paper bags. Any kind of paints, inks, crayons or markers can be used for drawing. Rubber cement is handy; if you stick something on your card and then change your mind, you can remove it easily.

Make a birthday invitation stencil by drawing a cartoon ...

and cutting it out.

Now use the stencil to paint the shape onto your paper.

RAINY DAY PARTY

When it's dry, add cartoon details with fine-point markers.

Cut out the character, leaving the card hinged on the folded sides. Open it up and write your message inside.

▲

Make a "shape" card. Draw a cartoon character. Trace it onto the top of your folded paper so that the edges form part of the character's outline.

◄ Create a comic card by drawing a cartoon on the front of the card . . .

► and *the* punch line inside *the* card.

TIP!

Sketch any drawings for your greeting cards on scrap paper first. Keep your good paper for the final product.

········· FLIP BOOKS

Bring your cartoon characters to life by drawing them in a flip book! A flip book has the same cartoon character on each page, but on each page, the position of the character changes slightly. When the pages are flipped, the character looks as if it is moving—just like the characters in animated movies.

Step One:

Here are three ways to make a flip book.

Staple together several pieces of paper 8 cm x 13 cm (3 x 5 inches). Keep the edges of the pages even.

OR

Stack several index cards and secure them together at one end with a sturdy elastic band.

OR

Use a small notepad that is already glued or bound on one side.

Step Two:

Plan how you want your character to move, and sketch the character's movement in a sequence of different positions.

Step Three:

Using a pencil, draw your character's first position on the last page of the book. Make sure you draw your character near the edge of the page so you'll be able to see it easily when you flip the pages.

Step Four:

Skip a few pages. Copy your character's second position onto this page. Continue in this way, drawing your character until you have drawn the final position. Then fill in the empty pages with the character's positions in sequence.

Step Five:

Test your flip book by flipping the pages from the back page to the front page. Revise any illustrations that make the character's movement look odd. Then trace over your pencil drawings with a fine-point black marker.

Here are some sample cartoon characters for you to practise drawing on the pages of a flip book.

Now dream up some cartoon flip books of your own.

POSTERS

Use your cartoon characters to announce events to the public. How? By drawing them on posters!

Plan your poster design. First make several rough designs on small pieces of scrap paper. Draw every idea you have—even the most wild or kooky. Anything goes while you're at this rough scribbling stage.

Review all your poster ideas and choose the design you like best.

If you plan to paint your poster, use heavy poster paper that won't buckle and pucker from the moisture of wet paint.

Now, following your rough design, draw your cartoon on a larger piece of scrap paper. Write any words quite large so that they can be read from a distance.

Tack your poster up on the wall and step back. Does the cartoon grab your eye? Can you easily read the words? When you're satisfied with your poster design, draw it on good poster paper.

When your poster is ready to be colored, photocopy it. Then you'll have another copy just in case you make a color mistake.

Decorate your poster with colored markers or poster paint. Paint with a brush or try different techniques. Dab on the paint with a sponge, or splatter on different colors with an old toothbrush. Be creative and try some special effects!

Add the lettering only when the paint and markers are completely dry. Now your cartoon poster is ready to make people stop and take notice!

 **TIP!** Wide-tip color markers and poster paints are great for coloring posters because they cover large areas easily.

MORE CARTOON PROJECTS

There are lots of other ways you can use your cartooning talents!

Use markers, water-color paint, oil paint and nail polish to turn odd-shaped rocks and pieces of wood into cartoon characters.

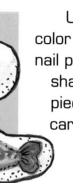

Use them as decorations, paper weights or bookends.

Draw cartoon characters on homemade book covers.

Make your own stationery by drawing cartoons on plain tablet paper and matching envelopes.

Make a cartoon T-shirt for yourself. Trace your design onto a light-colored or white T-shirt with pencil and then outline it in black laundry marker that won't wash out.

You can even buy fabric paints and fabric dyes to add color to your cartoon T-shirt.

During the holidays paint cartoons in holiday themes on your windows. Use poster paint; it washes off quite easily with warm, soapy water.

TIP! **Be sure to ask permission before painting, and don't forget to spread newspapers or old sheets on the floor to protect it from paint drops!**

You'll have a great time thinking of many more ways to display your cartoons. And remember—everyone loves cartoons, so be sure to share them. Happy cartooning!